SAYING IT RIGHT

A LANGUAGE AID FOR ADULTS

BY

MADGE MYERS CANTER

ISBN: 0-7596-9153-3

This book is printed on acid free paper.

1stBooks - rev. 02/05/02

THANKS

Many thanks to Claudia Marie Canter,
the baby boomer who helped;
and to Judith Frank Cox,
who encouraged me.

CONTENTS

PREFACE

BY THE AUTHOR

This work is not copyrighted. Feel free to duplicate any part of it and share with others. If you already know all you want to know about American English, you can turn to the "Greenwallisms" and figure out what the man was trying to say.

"Greenwallisms", as I have dubbed them, are not fictitious. In a number of other chapters, however, I have invented some dialogue to make a point. In the Contents you will see various topics, each one stemming from my theme of GOOD TALK.

In developing topics of this sort, a bit of humor is inevitable. I hope no one feels that I am making fun of him or her. My observations are practically all inspired by television.

After we become adults, our manner of speaking is more or less fixed. We do not expect to have our words corrected; that is, unless we have siblings. Brothers and sisters seem to feel free at any age to pounce on one another's grammar. The rest of us receive little if any instruction. Even our good friends refrain from offering help, fearing to hurt our feelings.

So how can we grown-ups know how good our speech is, or how bad? That's where this little book comes in. It can be used for self-help. And there is something in it for everybody. Enjoy!

PART ONE

THE "G" WORD

DOES IT MATTER?

How important is correct speech? Does it matter how we talk just so long as we are understood? We are adults, after all, and making a pretty good living. Why should we bother with a book like this?

Hons, as our Celia Rivenbark would address her readers, don't worry. Be happy.

But if you aspire to be a schoolteacher, or a lawyer, or a senator, or an evangelist, or a college president, or a speechwriter for the president of The United States, you know that correct English is very important, even essential.

Prince Charles visited this country some years ago and left with this comment: "Americans are becoming unintelligible." (Yes, yes, the British are often hard for us to understand.)

We don't want to become "unintelligible" to people of our mother country. We want to meet the standards of Professor Higgins. (Sorry, I can't believe I said that.) No doubt Professor H. would give up on most of us before we could "get" it.

We should talk more about language. Forget that we haven't been in a classroom in years. A renewed interest in grammar need not be academic.

MISCELLANEOUS

Have you heard about The Grammar Lady? Her name is Mary Newton Bruder, and she lives Mount Lebanon, Pennsylvania. She runs a kind of emergency hot line for questions about English grammar. The number as published in February of 1999 is 1-800-279-9708.

Dr. Bruder also has a Web site: www.grammarlady.com. She has an office, where she can be called Monday through Friday, nine to five.

Adults trying to understand references to movies will find it helpful to become familiar with quotations from *Casablanca* and *The Wizard of Oz.* The latter has been seen by nearly everyone, and we all know what it means to be told we are not in Kansas anymore.

It is valuable beyond measure to read a daily newspaper. Even if you can't "take it all in," you will learn bits and pieces that will add up. If the Sunday edition is too expensive for your budget, you can do well with just five workday issues.

An advice column, such as Ann Landers, can help in language study.

One of the TV talk shows might help a newcomer to this country. I hesitate to mention any, as I have not followed one in recent years. The Sunday Morning show on CBS is excellent; and I try not to miss Andy Rooney on Sixty Minutes, a prestigious TV magazine production.

Another matter of importance to a newcomer is how he or she wishes to be addressed. If you are new in a workplace and not comfortable being called by your first name, you can simply say pleasantly that you usually go by your last name. If your name is long or hard to pronounce, it would be a good thing to modify it to make it easy to say.

THE VERY WORST

Grammar is beyond some people. Bless their hearts, they simply don't get it. Fortunately it is quite possible to live a happy and successful life while "murdering" the King's English every day. As Patricia O'Conner said in her book *Woe Is I*, "This does not mean that we don't love you."

Let us consider the worst mistakes. One of them starts in childhood. We hear, "Me and Jimmy want to play." Then we hear the immediate correction: "Jimmy and I."

This is learned all too well. My daughter says it is probably the reason many adults use "I" when "me" is correct. They speak like this: "Is that for Mary and I?" "They left John and I off the list." "Please excuse Jane and I." "Are you going to invite Bob and I?" Bad grammar. "Me" is correct.

Ironically, the desire to be correct causes the error. To avoid this mistake, the speaker should mentally test the "I" in front of the name. He or she will think: Is that for I and Mary? They left I and John off the list. Please excuse I and Jane. Are you going to invite I and Bob? OF COURSE NO ONE TALKS LIKE THAT.

A classic example was given us inadvertently by our former President, William Jefferson Clinton, who was heard saying, "Your invitation to Hillary and I is most appreciated." As Kilpatrick would say, "Aarrgh!"

There is another test. QUESTION: Which is correct in these sentences? My brother is older than *me/I*. My mother thinks Aunt Polly is prettier than *her/she*. Our new neighbors seem to be richer than *us/we*. ANSWER: The verb is understood. Therefore we should think like this: *older than I am, prettier than she is, richer than we are.*

On second thought, my title is all wrong. These are not the "very worst" grammatical errors. Who is to say what they are. Perhaps "ain't" and "it don't" should head the list. But to me the mistakes made by college graduates and professional writers are the most inexcusable. These people are well-educated and should know better. We look to them to SAY IT RIGHT.

LIE and LAY, LYING and LAYING

Every day we hear LAY when it should be LIE. We hear LAYING when it should be LYING. This is not a matter of education. College graduates are heard making the same mistake.

There is a reason we do this. Many of us in childhood learned a bedtime prayer that started off "Now I lay me down to sleep." As adults we have heard in song the words, *Like a bridge over troubled water I will lay me down.*

Hey, you think, there's nothing ungrammatical about that—unless "myself" might be better than "me." You are right. But consider this: Without the "me" after "lay" would it be correct?

Consider LAY and LIE. The first is a <u>working</u> verb, the type called transitive. The other is called <u>intransitive</u>. We never have any trouble with the transitive LAY.

We lay bricks, we lay tile, we lay down the law, we lay things aside, and we lay the baby on the bed. LAY, LAYING, LAID… Never any trouble… Nobody gets it wrong.

But LIE? There's the trouble. LIE is constantly getting confused with LAY. Adding to the confusion, the past tense of LIE is the same as the present tense of LAY. Example: All day yesterday the twenty-dollar bill lay unnoticed in the ditch.

It does not help that we have an identical infinitive "TO LIE" meaning to tell an untruth. The "ing" forms are even the same. Example: "He is lying through his teeth" compared with "He is lying down to rest."

We have difficulty only with the word that means "to recline" or "to exist," as in "Somewhere in the evidence <u>lies</u> the truth." In the dictionary we see the principal parts: LIE, LYING, LAY, LAIN. We need to learn them.

LIKE LIKE LIKE

TOO MANY "LIKE's" in the title. Yes—and I am trying to make a point. The word "like" is used too much. The latest overuse took me by surprise. It is the habit of sprinkling meaningless "like's" throughout ordinary speech. Here is an example:

> *It was only like three o'clock, and no one was like hungry; but we decided to stop by this cafe that was like two blocks away. There were like a dozen people in the place. We chose a table by the window, where we could, like, people-watch.*

Have you noticed that the little word "as" is neglected these days? And "like" is taking over. The worst use is "LIKE I said." Everyone please repeat after me: "AS I SAID, AS I SAID, AS I SAID."

Also "as if" and "as though" are neglected. It is a relief to hear them occasionally instead of the constantly heard "like." The following are the introductory words that cause the trouble:

> *It looks, it seems, it sounds, it acts, it moves, it smells;*
>
> *He talks, he walks, he eats, he sings, he works, etc.*

Instead of "like" we should practice saying "as if" and "as though." Let's repeat these examples: IT LOOKS AS IF IT MIGHT RAIN; IT SEEMS AS THOUGH HE WANTS TO BE FIRED; IT SOUNDS AS IF THE MOTOR IS DYING; HE TALKS AS THOUGH HE'S THINKING OF RETIRING; HE WALKS AS IF HIS FEET HURT; HE EATS AS THOUGH HE'S ALMOST STARVED; HE SINGS AS IF HE MEANS EVERY WORD; HE WORKS AS THOUGH HE REALLY ENJOYS IT.

If you are fast-thinking, you can zap the "like" by saying "the way." For instance: The choir filed into the loft THE WAY it usually did.

More examples: The girl curtsied THE WAY her mother had taught her. The audience did not applaud THE WAY they usually did. The clowns did not act THE WAY he remembered them. The patient responded THE WAY the doctor expected. I was driving THE WAY I had been taught.

FINERPOINTS

No, I am not the doyenne of FOAL, an acronym for Friends of the American Language. Someone such as Patricia T. O'Conner would be perfect for the honor. Columnist James J. Kilpatrick would be a worthy vice-doyen.

My faults are known to myself, but I haven't overcome them yet. I hear myself saying "yeah"; I catch myself saying "I bet" when it is not appropriate for an elderly woman to use a gambling term; and I quite often use "kinda" and "sorta."

To my credit I am sparing with "okay" and "kids." Also I shrink from using "like" as in "I feel like he's trying to con us" and "It seems like he's always talking." The word "that" is what I use instead of "like."

Another effort I make is not to match "they", "them" and "their" with singular subjects. One of those subjects is very tricky. I am referring to "everybody." Doesn't that sound plural? To illustrate: A teacher asks, "Did everybody bring their lunch today?" The same teacher would say, "Is everybody here?" Never "Are everybody here?" The word is singular.

Colloquially the teacher is correct; but a stickler for exactness would ask, "Did everybody bring lunch today?" or "Did everybody bring his or her lunch today?"

Picky? Yes, and you can be picky yourself. Try reading the following:

> I do not use "impact" as a verb.
> I do not say "Aren't I?"
> I consider "unique" as never needing "very."
> "Nauseous" is the wrong word for "nauseated.".
> A souvenir is not a "momento." It's a "memento."
> The verb "to lay" should not be confused with "to lie."
> The "at" in "Where's it at?" is superfluous.

IMPERFECTIONS

MY own imperfections let me know how hard it is for all of us to break a habit. I still say "kinda" and "sorta." I still say "yeah" and "I bet." Sometimes I even hear myself saying, "Oh boy." That can date a person.

One imperfection I rid myself of years ago. I abruptly decided not to say, "Aren't I?" And it's been "Am I not?" ever since. I still hear "Aren't I?" spoken on TV, most notably by Barbara Walters and Candice Bergen.

I was twenty before I realized that I was saying, "Let's don't" instead of "Let's not." Not everyone catches his or her own mistakes. Many people go through life oblivious of their language imperfections. They get along quite well. They can be happy and successful. But others, such as young persons entering the work force, can be handicapped because of faulty speech.

Help with language should be available to anyone who seeks it. I believe it would be in the national interest to have free clinics. These could be implemented by local colleges. And shopping malls could provide the space. No money need be spent; everything would be voluntary.

BEFORE & AFTER

Like I said, he's not interested.	*As I said, he's not interested.*
Between you and I, he's a nut.	*Between you and me, he's a nut.*
I bet he'll be late.	*I feel sure he'll be late...*
He talks like he's giving up.	*He talks as though he's giving up.*
If I was him, I'd stay put.	*If I were he, I'd stay put.*
Why don't you lay down and rest?	*Why don't you lie down and rest?*

THE FORMAL FIVE

Five of the following are in formal English. Which are they?

1. My predecessor was older than me.
2. Me and Jimmy want to go out to play.
3. The house looks different than I remember.
4. Where's your office at?
5. Did everyone remember to bring his or her passport?
6. Well, sir, it looks like you owe a bundle.
7. What do you think of me adding an extra room?
8. Everyone must fasten their seatbelt.
9. I'm sure I seen it first.
10. The documents were found in the mayor's desk.
11. Everything seems to be okay.
12. I wish I was in Vegas tonight.
13. How come you didn't call 911?
14. Better get them boxes out of the way.
15. The newspaper was found lying in a puddle of water.
16. I don't know where they had went before coming here.
17. Mother, you should lay down and rest for a while.
18. The baby was found laying on the bed, sound asleep.

19. She walked in like she owned the place.
20. It was a long flight, and everybody on the plane was tired.
21. His argument is very persuasive, but I don't buy it.
22. Did you know they hung Tom Dooley?
23. Like I said, the kids have a hard time spelling such words.
24. Like my father said, nobody learns anything while talking.
25. At the conclusion of the service, the family left quietly.

WHAT NEWCOMERS WILL HEAR

Newcomers will hear American English spoken correctly and incorrectly. They will have to figure out the difference. The trouble is that many native residents of the United States are—as we say of pianists—playing it by ear.

It is too late to go back to school, and in most instances the person with poor speech skills is unaware of his deficiency. A newcomer from a privileged background will understand this and make allowances.

It should be helpful to a newcomer to have a list of common imperfections that he can avoid. Below is a partial list:

TEACHER: Bring this note home to your mother. (take)

PASSENGER: I feel nauseous. (nauseated)

EMPLOYER: Irregardless of your lack of experience, we will hire you. (regardless)

PHYSICIAN: You must eat healthy foods. (healthful)

SALESMAN: Like I said, it's a real bargain. (As I said)

PHOTOGRAPHER: It don't matter. Your shoes won't show.

(It doesn't matter)

NEIGHBOR: Between you and I, this neighborhood has gone down.(Between you and me)

DETECTIVE: The chalk shows where the body was laying. (lying)

METEOROLOGIST: Looks like showers will continue. (as if)

BANK OFFICER: The stock market has impacted our rates. (has had an impact on)

COLLEGE STUDENT: Mom and Dad, what do you guys think of my going to Europe this summer? (you, or "you two" instead of "you guys")

BOYFRIEND: Indisposed! What is that supposed to mean? (What does that mean?)

REPORTER: Is this the tree where the victim was hung? (hanged)

FASHION DESIGNER: I'm good, aren't I? (am I not?)

NEW WORKER: It's a lousy job and the pay stinks. (hard job, low pay)

PRONUNCIATION

Nobody looks up pronunciation more often than I do. There are troublesome words that have bothered me, and I have returned to the dictionary several times to reassure myself. "Lingerie" is one of these words. I hear that "ray" sound at the end, and I can't understand why I don't hear "ree." A surprise happened yesterday. On Guiding Light, "lingerie" was pronounced my way by the actress who plays Reva Shayne. I was delighted. But if a vote were taken, I am sure that "ray" would win. We like words from the French, and if we Americanize them, that's not so bad.

The same with another word of French origin, "harassment." We usually hear the RASS stressed. The late Sydney J. Harris in one of his columns wrote that "harass" should be stressed on the first syllable. Popular custom, however, has settled on "ha-RASS-ment; and my dictionary now gives it first. The same thing is happening to "minuscule."

When a mispronunciation causes a confusion of meaning, however, we should resist it. I am thinking of "forte." There is an inclination to say "fortay." I am not referring to the musical term meaning "loud," but to the word for special talent or strong point. "Forte" should be one syllable, like "fort." We should not say "for-tay.".

Our English language tends to stress the first syllable, and this tendency causes some amusing mispronunciations. Three examples favored by "rednecks" are: MO-tel, PO-lice, and GUI-tar…

Vowel sounds can differ from region to region. The strangest to me is this: "pank and grain" for "pink and green."

Does "Betta not be late for the weddin" sound like you? If so, you need to work on final "g" and "r." Hearing ourselves on tape can be a revelation, and first step toward improvement. Not many of us can talk like Charles Osgood of *Sunday Morning* fame, but listening to him could help train our ear to recognize excellent tone and pronunciation.

THREE SHORT EXERCISES

Read aloud the two columns. Which one sounds like you?

COLUMN A	COLUMN B
singa’	singer
pitcha’	pitcher
proppa’	proper
motha’	mother
fatha’	father
nevva’	never
sista’	sister
huntin’	hunting
gettin’	getting
skatin’	skating
readin’	reading
racin’	racing
puttin’	putting
feedin’	feeding
Car’lina	Carolina
Flor’da	Florida
Wash’ton	Washington
Col’rado	Colorado
Mar’land	Maryland
Cal’fornia	California
Al’bama	Alabama

A NAME AND A NUMBER

Names are important. We start life with a name and a hospital bracelet. Our identification is assured. If we happen to be saddled with a name we don't like, we can do something about it when we are older. In the United States it is good to have a name which can be pronounced easily, without a string of syllables. In my opinion, five or six syllables should be enough for anybody, and a limit of a dozen letters.

For example, a White House press secretary some years ago had the Greek name Stephanopolis. Thirteen letters. Not too many sounds, but one too many letters. How easy it would have been to shorten the name to Stevens. Or Stephenson.

A name can now be backed up by a number, our SSN, initials for Social Security Number. It is formed of nine digits: three-two-four. Some day we may all be wearing "dog tags." with our SSN on them. Our proper names alone are not completely reliable as a means of protecting our identity.

My own last name is Canter. Simple enough? No. I get "Carter" quite often. Madge is my given name, and I get Marge. I'm thankful for my SSN.

First names seem to be getting out of control, as witness birth announcements. I found these in the Myrtle Beach Sun News: Tarteskikar, Latrajai Qa'Toria, Di'Sheak Gennaro, Jaheim Le'Terruis, and

Destasia Hi'Sheanna. These poor babies are going to be called by initials, as "Miss T" or "Mr. D."

We have done well with Spanish names, though at first we had difficulty with sports figures, especially baseball players. But soon the easier names came naturally to us. Who does not remember fondly the late Roberto Clemente?

A name. We like to hear it pronounced right, and when we see it in print, we want it spelled right. Also we have a number, and we know to get it just right. We have an identity. We are unique—one of a kind. And that in itself is sort of wonderful.

YOU NEED HELP

Help is what you need if you talk like this:

I like to died.
He don't know no better.
Yeah, man, I done taken my pill.
She don't know where it's at.
We don't buy that idea. It's lousy from the get-go.

I think I'm getting nauseous.
The company went belly up.
Ain'tcha got no decaf?
We had went there many times. It's a swell place.
You could care less about me printing that story.

That plan sucks.
Like I said, it's really him.
Between you and I, that new soft drink will never fly.
I seen the money laying on the table.
I'm going to be invited, aren't I?

If I was you, I'd stay away from them gangs.
The party was neat, and the little honoree quite cool.
Ladies, what would you guys like to order?
Do you think wine at dinner is healthy?
They were sittin' at the table but not eatin' anything.

PRACTICE SENTENCES

TO BE READ ALOUD

1. If I were you, I would not do that.
2. If you were I, what would you do?
3. If I were she, I would not do that.
4. If I were he, I would not do that.
5. Do you think it is she?
6. No, it's not she. It's he.
7. As I said, it wasn't I.
8. Do you think it was she?
9. If we were they, we would not do that.
10. As the forecast said, it rained.
11. He looks as though he's pleased.
12. They act as though they own the place.
13. I feel as if I might faint.
14. It seems as if everything is working out.
15. She walks as if her feet are hurting.
16. As they told us, the store was closed.
17. As we expected, nobody was at home.
18. As everyone hoped, the skater did not fall.
19. As I was saying, it's nobody's fault.
20. She acts as though she doesn't believe us.
21. Nobody thinks that he or she is boring.
22. Each person waited to hear his or her name called.
23. Everybody had already made up his mind.

24. Has everybody found his right place?
25. Every bride wants her wedding to be nice.
26. Somebody has failed to sign his application.

PART TWO

SAY WHAT?

YOUR VOCABULARY

Do words fascinate you? Do you prize your dictionary? Have you figured out the diacritical marks?

The what? The tiny marks over the vowels to indicate the way we say the alphabet, or broadened, as the "a" in "ah." Then there is the little slanty mark that tells which syllable to accent. Down in the right-hand corner of the page we see examples. A magnifying glass will come in handy for this.

We discover that the short sounds have no mark over them. This short vowel sound is unfamiliar to Hispanics and gives them trouble. That is why we hear "eet" for "it." Fortunately it is not hard to understand if we hear "Eet ees gued."

The consonants are given attention inside the front cover, with key words that would be helpful to foreigners brushing up on their English. As I have mentioned in a previous chapter, my dictionary is Webster's New World Dictionary of American English, third college edition c. 1989.

How good is your vocabulary? Pretty good, I would think, if half of the words in this random list have meaning for you: *eponymous, hyperbole, indigenous, pernicious, insidious, obsequious, recalcitrant, plethora, interstices, expound, cynosure, disparity, askance, awry, cowl, retinue, facetious, levity, execrable, fortuitous, rigorous, austere.*

If you are willing to look up words, you will find plenty in an epic novel by Hervey Allen, *Anthony Adverse.* Your public library will have it. It is historical fiction that will appeal to both sexes.

The late Taylor Caldwell is another novelist whom I would mention for vocabulary enrichment. And a book by the late James M. Michener would be a language gold mine.

SLANG and COLLOQUIALISMS

Slang is welcome in most households, but it has to use the back door. We let it in because it can be fun. I smile every time I hear "laid-back." For a fleeting moment I hear Jimmy Buffet singing *Margaritaville.* Teachers are expected to discourage slang, but they are often heard using it themselves.

And everybody enjoys colloquialisms. These expressions, as well as slang, can be confusing to the uninitiated; but they are how we communicate with one another on a daily basis.

We understand, however, that slang and colloquialisms are unsuitable in certain situations. On the witness stand we are told to answer Yes or No—not Yeah or Nope. And we do not hear a presiding judge say, "Okay."

A cop series called *Due South* featured a Canadian mountie who spoke formal English. He never said "Okay." He said, "Understood." His language was always formal, even erudite. Most unusual. And we loved hearing him. Oratory may be unfashionable today, but we still find delight in our great language when we hear it at its best.

Colloquial speech is about all that most of us can manage, and some do better with it than others. There is a talent, I believe, for speech. Intelligence seems to go along with the glibness. Many of our young people have both talent and intelligence. If they are motivated, they can achieve a mastery of English to equal that of the *Due South* mountie.

Slang is not understood by everybody. Not everybody knows "snafu," but a President once used it on television. Another former President said he was "out of the loop," and I wondered if he meant Chicago. Better for high officials to use formal language, is it not? Less possibility of causing a misunderstanding.

Usually foreigners have trouble with our idioms and fad words, and we have trouble with theirs. Let us all be patient and helpful.

ARE WE "COOL"?

A teen-ager named Kim once commented to her parents that I was a real cool lady. It was one of the best compliments I ever had. I think it meant she liked me. This word "cool" is exceedingly popular as a term of approval, and it has been picked up by many adults.

Is this bad? Yes and no. As slang goes, "Cool" is a gem. It even has a partner, "Neat." If one won't work, the other will. For instance, if the Grand Canyon defies the word "cool," it can be described as "neat." These two words are modern equivalents of "Swell"—the top slang word of the '20s and '30s.

On second thought, the young set has a third superlative, "awesome," and it would be perfect for the Grand Canyon. These three adjectives will more than likely be popular for a long time.

Some of us are convinced that slang and fad words do harm to our thought processes. Certainly we are concerned about vocabulary growth. In this regard I can suggest a strategy, one that calls for a real effort on our part.

Whenever "cool" is heard, the person in charge will ask what kind of "cool" is meant; then offer a variety of descriptive words to choose from. For instance, these adjectives come to mind: *admirable, bold, powerful, masterful, clever, heroic, talented, charming, entertaining, imaginative,* and *generous.* A selection should also be ready for "neat" and "awesome."

We may need to consult a dictionary. Children like to hear new words. Remember the commercial that had a father saying he was skeptical, and the little boy said that he was "skepital too"? Instead of talking down to a child, it could benefit us all to try out a few five-dollar words.

All this is a neat idea, *n'est-ce pas?* Quite awesome. We are COOL!

"YOU GUYS" and "YOU ALL"

How did this get started? I am referring to the use of "you guys" in addressing both males and females. Why men accept this, and why women also accept this, is beyond my understanding. Perhaps they never saw the hit play and movie "Guys and Dolls." "Guys" meant the males. Also, the phrase "a 'guy' thing" is sometimes used to refer to something peculiar to the male sex. It makes no sense to say "you guys" to a group of ladies.

James J. Kilpatrick says that there is nothing we can do about "you guys." He feels that the habit is too "ingrained." I don't agree. If enough fuss is made about it, and enough fun is made of it, it will go away. In the unisex use, that is.

Wait a minute, you Northerners say. What about "you all"? We have made friendly fun of "you all" for generations, and it certainly hasn't gone away. It must be ingrained, as Mr. Kilpatrick said about "you guys."

Actually, I believe we Southerners are saying "you all" less often than we used to. And we never address one person as "you all." It is always used in the plural. Call it an invention of sorts, to fill the need for a second-person plural pronoun.

What do the British say? They might suggest using the third person, as in "Would your lordships care to order now?" (Just kidding.)

"You all" comes easily to Anne George, author of the Southern Sisters mysteries. Her sleuthing characters say "you all" all day long. Usually it is shortened to "Y'all." It is a regional thing.

Regional expressions are fine, but we Americans move about. We find ourselves in a different region. We are not in Kansas anymore. That is why we should be willing to adapt quickly to differences. A new friend can be very helpful. There is nothing wrong in asking for some tutoring.

YOU GUYS and YOU ALL. Neither is perfect. But they are what we have until the arbiters of English come up with the perfect compromise.

EXAMPLES of avoiding "you all" and "you guys":

1. Will you Board members please be seated.
2. Where are you vacationers from?
3. You scouts wait for me right here.
4. I don't want you ladies to be caught in the rain.
5. These instructions are for you folks.
6. We thank you parents and guardians for coming out tonight.
7. There is a message for you workers on the bulletin board.
8. Are you campers having a good time?
9. This compliment is for you people in the balcony.
10. You children must get quiet and go to sleep.
11. Have you guests found everything you need?
12. You nurses are much admired by many people.
13. We couldn't have done this without you volunteers.
14. You three have been chosen to lead the parade.
15. What have you Joneses been doing this year?
16. The fish are biting. You sportsmen hurry on down.
17. I have some good news for all you stockholders.
18. I'll never forget you neighbors.
19. You two make a lovely couple.

Madge Myers Canter

IMAGERY

We have all been admonished not to mix metaphors; but when have we been advised not to use them at all! Lately I have heard *Get on the horn, We are not on the same page,* and *Does that ring a bell?*

Someone else complains that all his hard work has gone *down the toilet*. Another person warns that soon the whole story will *hit the fan.* A few minutes later we hear the advice to *get your ducks in a row.*

We have a way with words. We are imaginative and clever, and we enjoy projecting pictures with our words. We use cliches, such as *the tip of the iceberg* or *the light at the end of the tunnel.* Great old metaphors, but worn out from overuse. Oh, for some fresh ones!

He's a chip off the old block. This is another gem. I wonder who first said that. It must have been around for centuries. For me it evokes a memory of my Uncle Tom Martin swinging an axe as he split firewood for my grandmother's cookstove. Nowadays not many children have seen (or smelled) a pile of wood chips lying around a huge chopping block. Why not just say, "He's a lot like his father."

I sound cranky. When have I ever originated a clever expression? Actually, I have tried. What I came up with was *She's a few feathers short of a boa.* Well, you try it. It's not easy.

Would you dare say *I didn't just fall off a turnip truck*? (Well, Lisa said it on As the World Turns.) At least the image of a turnip truck is somehow amusing. And as far as I know, it is a fairly new expression. We like to be up-to-date. For example, we no longer say *a one-horse town;* we say *a one-stoplight town.*

Imagery! How wonderful that pictures can be flashed on our minds by words. Not all pictures, however, are effective. They can distract us. We would do well to exercise care in what we put on the "screen." Just plain language is often the best. What do you think?

SUFFERING FROM POPULARITY

Patricia T. O'Conner has advised writers not to use worn-out expressions. She gives a list of them with humorous comments in her book about good writing, *WOE IS I.* Mrs. O'Conner is an editor for The New York Times.

Examples from her list are: *LET'S GET THE SHOW ON THE ROAD; BUG GOING AROUND; BOTTOM LINE; DIAMOND IN THE ROUGH; EASIER SAID THAN DONE; GLASS CEILING; LEVEL PLAYING FIELD;* and *PUSHING THE ENVELOPE.*

I am adding a few of my own: IT DOESN'T RING A BELL; A LOT ON MY PLATE RIGHT NOW; WE ARE ON THE SAME PAGE; WORKING MY—OFF; A PAIN IN THE—; GET ON THE BALL; BIOLOGICAL CLOCK; BALLPARK FIGURE; WHAT GOES AROUND COMES AROUND; and LIGHT AT THE END OF THE TUNNEL.

Come on, you can help me. What about these: CUT TO THE CHASE; DON'T RAIN ON MY PARADE; PULL OUT ALL THE STOPS; STOP TO SMELL THE ROSES; SHORT END OF THE STICK; SWEATING BULLETS; and LAST AS LONG AS A SNOWBALL IN HELL. Also IN THE FAST LANE, and MOTHER-IN-LAW FROM HELL.

But wait a minute, you complain. After we see the O'Conner list of cliches, what is left to say? We love those old expressions.

This is a free country. You can talk any way you like—unless, of course, you fall out of a raft and curse a blue streak in front of children. Remember the news item? Ordinarily, though, we can talk the way we want to.

Would we be too dull, however, if we just spoke plainly with no attempt to show off our cleverness? Those hearing us might find it refreshing.

GREENWALLISMS

He did not know that the office workers were compiling his sayings. They were secretive. After all, Mr. Greenwall was the manager. From my copy I have selected the following for your amusement:

Participation in the form of rain or snow
Many centurions not in nursing homes

Toll-free checking	Prompt and ceremony
Drum and Broadstreet	Bear the blunt of it
Can't phantom why	State of the ark
Autobomb in Germany	One of my cohards
Acting nonshellac	Wheels on meals
A good work ethnic	One-shop stopping
K-Mark and Wal-mark	Running an optical course
Fill a voyage	Golf coast of Florida
Wait with baited hook	A doubled-barreled sword
Work resentlessly	Let's all be in the same sink

Crutch of the matter
Impeaching upon someone's rights
Grass seeds movement

EXCLAMATIONS

Exclamations pose a problem. In the early years of television Jack Benny could get a laugh simply by saying, "Well!" The rest of us, however, seem to need a variety of expressions. The first we learned at toddler age was probably "Uh-oh." To this day that one portends something not good.

The second exclamation we said as a child may have been "Ouch." And the third, "Goody." Of course this is not a scientific study.

As we grow older we find that exclamations are not always mild and inoffensive. They can be a matter of concern. "God!" is one of them. To many people this word sounds like breaking a Commandment. This is why we have so many euphemisms.

But not everyone approves of these euphemisms. Some years ago *dog-gone* was heard quite often, but after word got around that it meant *god-damn,* it dropped from use. In more recent years another questionable exclamation has come to notice, and that is "Jeez." I don't like to hear it.

An old expression surfaced the other day. I told Marie that high schools did not have wrestling. "Shoot fire," she said, "Wilkes Central did."

It is hard to say why some euphemisms are more acceptable than others. Let's review a few: *good gracious, golly, gosh, mercy, my goodness, my lord, dear lord, good heavens, lord god...*

"Gomer Pyle" of a popular TV series amused his viewers with his drawling "Goll…y!" "Charlie Brown", of the comic strip Peanuts, expressed his frustrations and won our sympathy with his "Good grief!"

What else is there? We go to the funny papers again and find: *rats, yikes, zowie, wow, ee-e-eek, whee, whew, o-o-o-ps,* and *ouch.* Not much help in this matter.

"Oh boy" is dated. We hardly ever hear it anymore—but if you should win a lottery, what better exclamation is there than "OH BOY!"

THE SENSITIVE EAR

How many times have we heard "What is that supposed to mean?" when "What does that mean?" is all that was needed. "Supposed to" expresses scorn and disbelief, as a person might respond upon seeing a strange painting or sculpture.

We settle into patterns of speech. After awhile we don't hear ourselves. It is possible that the writers of soaps rarely listen to their finished product. They are busy going on to their next assignment.

The job of writers is to entertain and keep the ratings up. They are not paid to educate. But they are in a position to do so. When they combine entertainment with education, the viewers love it. What else accounts for the popularity of "West Wing?"

With all its awards, however, "West Wing" is vulnerable. I must mention a deplorable choice of words. It happened on two episodes. The writer had need of a word such as these: *offended, irritated, angered, annoyed, disturbed, displeased, tormented, plagued, et cetera.*

He chose none of these words. He chose "pissed off."

I'll never understand it. Did no one care enough to edit the word out before it aired on prime time? Is tolerance for vulgarity confused with sophistication?

Another vulgar word assaulted the ears more recently. A young actress on "All My Children" said "freaking."

What is going on? Will we all be better off to become desensitized? Will we enjoy our new-found sophistication?

Sensitive ears. Intelligent response. If we don't like what we are hearing, we can speak up. It's time.

FOUR- LETTER WORDS

Four-letter words, along with three and five-letter ones, have given us a vocabulary of which some people seem quite fond. Other people, however, find these words totally unacceptable.

We call them dirty words, some dirtier than others. My dictionary labels them "vulgar." Yes, they are all in my dictionary. As I have mentioned elsewhere, my dictionary is *WEBSTER'S NEW WORLD DICTIONARY, third college edition* 1984. (My daughter says it should be rated R.)

I have heard that there are seven words specifically banned from newspapers, and possibly from radio and television. I don't know what all seven are, but I have come across some raw expressions in bestsellers.

Here in Myrtle Beach we have an elegant theater called The Palace. One evening a handsome British singer found his audience unresponsive to his jokes. Soon they began to walk out. When the manager questioned them, they complained about the language.

Obviously the so-called Bible Belt is not the best venue for trying out raunchy material.

The late Victor Borge also appeared at The Palace. No bad language. I have read that Borge never in his long career ever used off-color patter.

A little child can say a naughty word, and people will laugh. When an adult does this, it is not funny.

Foreigners need to be aware of this. Like the child, they may not know the meaning of the word. Someone may have taught it to them as a prank.

I recall Reinie, a young man from Hamburg, who arrived at our complex quite confident of his high school English. He was sitting with Marie and me out by the pool, and writing down an address, when he dropped his pencil. To my astonishment he uttered an expletive. And for such a petty thing!

We ignored it. It is quite possible that a prank had been played on Reinie. Reprehensible, isn't it, to teach bad words to the unsuspecting. Shame!

EUPHEMISMS

I was reading a Jan Karon novel about a priest, and I wondered what he would say when he needed to let off steam. As it turned out, the good man said, "Blast!" Perhaps his seminary training had taught him that word, but I doubt that "blast" will ever put "damn" out of business.

"Damn" and "Hell" seem to be the swear words heard most often on television. On the daytime drama *All My Children,* a lawyer named Jack Montgomery is constantly provoked into asking, "What in hell is going on?"

There are many ways of using the "hell" word: *What the hell, who in hell, where in hell, how in hell, why in hell, a hell of a mess, for the hell of it, from hell,* and *Go to hell.* The usual euphemism for "hell" is "heck," although my daughter's childhood piano teacher, who would never have dreamed of saying "Hell", pronounced the backstage area at a recital as "Hot as Hades."

In fictitious roles, women as well as men have said "damn" and "hell," but in real life women are considered "rough" if they swear. Rhett Butler did not give "a damn," but Scarlett would have had to settle for not giving a "fiddle-dee-dee." A double standard? Yes. It does not matter, however, as females have a whole bundle of expressions they can use which males consider too feminine to use themselves.

This topic finds me wading in deep water, but let's splash on. For instance, in *The Wizard of Oz* young Dorothy exclaims, "Lions, tigers and bears! Oh my!" We don't hear males saying "Oh my!" The character of Erica on *All My Children* uses the expression "My goodness!" a lot, but you don't often hear a male say that. In an old Shirley Temple movie, the little moppet says "My goodness!" and nobody minds. In Angela Lansbury's murder mysteries, Jessica Fletcher exclaims, "Good Lord!" and it sounds right. I recall hearing an acquaintance utter "Gosh darn!" It surprised me, but sounded oddly comforting in the hospital setting in which we found ourselves.

Euphemisms serve a purpose.

IS SPANISH OUR "OTHER" LANGUAGE?

SI, si. Yes, yes. One has only to look at labels to see Spanish along with English. And it's not a bad thing. Spanish is an excellent choice for a second language. It has been on our doorstep for centuries—or should I say our "back" doorstep. Our relationship with Mexico has not always been cordial, but it has improved greatly in recent years.

And nobody has ever said that Spanish is not a beautiful language.

It was a beautiful melody that inspired me to learn some Spanish. It was *La Golondrina* (the swallow). It began: *Adonde ira veloz y fatigada la golondrina que de aqui se va...* Even more lovely, I thought, than *La Paloma* (the dove). Both songs are from Mexico.

Spanish is a much older language than English. Compared with Spanish, and also French and Italian, English is the new kid on the block. In fact, there was a time when it was disdained at the royal court in London. French was spoken instead.

In the early seventeenth century, however, the English language came into its own with the works of William Shakespeare and the monumental King James version of *The Holy Bible*.

Spanish and English are quite different, needless to say. Spanish flows more leisurely. English takes shortcuts. We say "John's book." They say *"el libro de Juan."* And every noun is either masculine or feminine!

The Hispanics among us have come with Spanish as their native tongue. Many of them speak English quite well. It is a remarkable accomplishment, as English is not easy to learn. We have no idea how confusing our English can be to foreigners.

SAYING IT RIGHT is my title. Can it involve two languages? More than likely I am overstepping. Certainly we don't expect everybody to become bilingual. But it's a thought, isn't it?

PART THREE

THE GIFT OF GAB

SMALL TALK

What is small talk? You may have never heard the expression, but it is in the dictionary. At least "small talk" appears in my dictionary, which, as I have said, has everything. It means light conversation. Nothing important.

Any two persons, or several persons, can engage in small talk. It helps to pass the time. I shall attempt to give an example: The scene is a waiting room. The characters are two strangers, an important-looking white man in his sixties, and a young, dark-complexioned woman.

He: Would you like a magazine?
She: No, thank you. My eyes are tired.
He: Have you been waiting long?
She: About forty minutes, but I don't mind. I hardly ever get to sit and do nothing.
He: You have a hard job?
She: Not too hard, but little time off. I have to be alert all the time.
He: Sounds important.
She: You could say that. You probably hold an important position.
He: I used to. I'm retired now.
She: My father had to take early retirement. But he keeps busy.

He: How does he do that? Does he play golf?
She: (laughing) Surely you jest. He tutors slow students. Today, though, he's taking over for me.
He: Now you've got me curious. May I ask what kind of work you do? But now they are calling my name. Aren't you next before me?
She: Oh, no. I'm just waiting for Arthur. He's my husband. After he takes care of you, we are going out to dinner. Nice talking with you.

Small talk can relieve the tedium of many situations. There is a variety of safe topics: the weather, the news, sports, traffic, food, inflation, etc.

SMOOTH TALK

Smooth talk is usually easy to recognize. You need to be cautious about making a decision when a smooth talker turns on the charm. He or she can be glib with the rosy outlook. We hear of the elderly being sold products they don't need, just to please a friendly, eager salesperson.

Years ago we had "traveling salesmen." They rode the trains, and stayed in a town only so long as the pickings were good. Sometimes women fell in love with them. According to old silent movies it was the smooth talk that women fell for.

Not every smooth talker is dishonest or insincere. A person of integrity with a talent for speaking can succeed in many fields, among them politics, law, evangelism, advertising, writing and teaching.

But the general conception of a "smooth talking man" is that he is deceptive and seductive. We can imagine him coming on to the landlady's daughter thusly: "Young lady, you certainly would turn heads in St. Louis. It's a shame you have never been there. I'd deem it an honor to show you the nightlife. You would love the theaters. In fact, you would look good up on a stage yourself."

He has her attention now. "In this here little town a beautiful young lady like you is like a flower born to bloom unseen, to waste its fragrance on the desert air."

In a few short minutes he has the girl thinking of her hometown as a veritable desert.

In our present time it is still hard for many people to resist a smooth talker. He or she is beguiling. The temptation to follow the piper is strong.

Parents want to hold their children close, to protect them from harm; but beyond the front yard lies a risky big world. The smooth talker is out there.

SWEET TALK

Sweet talk is personal, but that's no reason to leave it out of *SAYING IT RIGHT.* As far as I know, no one is an authority on this subject; so I'll put in my two cents worth.

The best setting for sweet talk is where there is a baby. Some people would disagree, but I see no harm in it. The baby has a name, of course, but he or she will learn it soon enough. Now is the time to indulge oneself in unrestrained flattery for that helpless infant. The little darling will inspire you. In a low, caressing voice you can say or sing almost anything. The tone is what matters. Remember Murphy Brown trying to sing to Avery? Sweet talk didn't come naturally to her, but she improvised.

The most basic word is "Baby." It goes well with "Sweet" and can be useful throughout life. If you call your husband or your wife "Sweet Baby", you likely are in a happy marriage. Let's list some classics: *darling, honey, sweetheart, sugar, precious, doll, sweetie pie, honey bun, sugar baby, dear heart,* and *love.* Of them all, the easiest and simplest to say, and most acceptable in public, is *DEAR.* Out in public is not the best place for using words of affection.

Many men are tongue-tied when it comes to sweet talk. It embarrasses them to say the words. The best they can do is buy a pretty card to speak for them.

Perhaps some day they can loosen up. Usually they don't mind being on the receiving end of sweet talk—in private, that is.

As I was growing up, my brothers and I did not hear sweet talk. Everyone was called by name. One summer we vacationed with our parents at Lake Waccamaw. A middle-aged couple joined us for the week. When the husband called his wife "Precious," we children thought it was hilarious.

Each to his taste, but now I think there is a time and place for sweet talk.

The sweetest I ever heard was in a nursing home. A young black nurse was tending to an old man. I found myself listening as her tender words flowed. She certainly had a talent. She should be recruited to teach a course.

PLAIN TALK

Plain talk, also called straight talk, is not always pleasing to hear. "To speak plainly," a lawyer might say, "you don't have a case."

Sometimes plain talk is necessary. If possible we try to soften it.

EXAMPLES

I'm sorry to have to tell you this, but we have to let you go.

The test is positive, so we must consider what measures to take.

The engagement is off. I am not going to marry you. It's over.

The loan has been denied. We are very sorry we can't help you.

There was a little accident. My fault. The car was totaled.

You must take your son out of our school. He does not fit in.

You are very sweet and pretty, but you don't have any talent.

My Aunt Pearl is coming to visit for two weeks. She's fun.

I forgot to pick up the dry cleaning. Please don't be mad.

We are so sorry, but your speaker has the flu and must cancel.

Are you sitting down? Your stocks just took a tumble.

The good news is you won; the bad, the company is bankrupt.

We have power, but cable is out. Tonight you'll miss the game.

SHOPTALK

Shoptalk is the specialized language used when people in the same line of work get together. It can lead to the exchange of important ideas. Or it can be a time-passer for a workaholic type.

Doctors, for instance, are in a world of their own when two or more engage in eager conversation. *Northern Exposure* viewers will recall young Dr. Fleischmann and how starved he was for the company of a fellow physician. Understanding his need, the bush pilot Maggie flew him to a distant Alaskan clinic where she left him for an hour-long visit with a kindred spirit.

We think of shoptalk taking place after hours, away from the workplace. Many a hostess has said, "Enough shoptalk now," her desire being to introduce a topic of general interest. By its nature, shoptalk is exclusive.

If you are confused as to what shoptalk really is, I should clarify it by stating some things it is not: it is not small talk; it is not gossip; it is not airing grievances; it is not serious discussion of company policy; and it's not planning a surprise party for the boss.

In the narrowest sense we might say that shoptalk is about the nuts and bolts of the job itself. It's about which method seems to work best; which supplies are more dependable; where the best equipment can be found; and where the new appliances can be installed.

Work talk, that's what it is. Work talk after hours, casual and pleasant. It is good, however, to cut it out when an outsider says, "Enough!"

BACK TALK

Back talk is not good. As children we learn not to talk back to our parents. One too many "Why?" and they lose patience. A surly "I don't want to" can bring punishment.

As grown-ups we can be tempted to talk back to an employer, but we know we might be fired. We must show respect.

Back talk shows disrespect. A colloquial synonym for it is "sassing."

Early in life we learn that our parents and other adults expect politeness.

Even an argumentative attitude can be considered disrespectful. When a son or daughter whines, "But everybody else is doing it," it borders on impudence.

There are situations, sad to say, when an adult does not deserve respect. In the strictest sense, a parent, however remiss, should be spoken to with courtesy. This calls for extreme patience and control.

Viewers of *All My Children* have watched as daughter Hayley was driven to disassociating herself from Arlene, an alcoholic. It was painful to hear Haley's harsh denunciation. In the same show, Dr. David Hayward speaks coldly to Vanessa, refusing to call her "Mother." And in *Guiding Light* the estranged Michelle Santos orders her biological mother, Claire

Ramsey, out of the house. Scenes like these are dramatic, but leave one feeling uncomfortable.

Generally, all back talk is bad. It is hurtful. Here are some examples:

> I'll do it when I get good and ready.
> You don't know what you're talking about.
> John's parents let him stay out till one o'clock.
> I'm watching television. I'll do it later.
> Why should I have to do everything!
> Why can't you get someone else to do it?
> That's not fair. Lots of girls start dating at fourteen.
> These vegetables are yucky. I want some hotdogs.
> You can't make me. I'm nearly eighteen.
> Mow the lawn yourself, old man. I'm going somewhere.
> My room is the way I like it. I'll clean it tomorrow.

CONFUSING TALK

Confusing talk has to be translated. This is second nature for many people but difficult for others. I am thinking of foreigners trying to learn English, and also our native-born unfamiliar with colloquialisms, fad words and slang. Our young children are among the latter group.

In consideration for those who will be puzzled by new words and phrases we should speak plainly when in their presence. The following sentences are examples of confusing talk.

It's a pretty bad situation. I don't buy their explanation.

What's with you guys? You know that plan won't fly.

It will cost an arm and a leg. Let's scuttle the whole shebang.

Did the cat get your tongue? This shyness drives me bonkers.

Everybody is expected to fish or cut bait.

This is a neat offer. Now the ball is in your court.

They have fallen head over heels in love.

They bit off more than they could chew. It's all gone south.

It's a job from hell. I'm swimming with sharks all day.

The train has left the station. We dropped the ball.

The students are beefing about the beefed-up rules.

Rumors can get started by confusing talk. Remember who is listening.

COMPLIMENTS

A compliment can be a joy forever. We treasure the memory of a very special one. The best are sincere and spontaneous and lift the spirits of the recipient. A person needs at least one compliment a day.

Every day we should compliment somebody on something. There are people who do this, and more, effortlessly. It is in their nature. Many more people, I am sorry to say, hardly ever say a kind word. They are stingy.

Yes, it is a stinginess. Oh no, YOU are not stingy. You give generously of your money—even your TIME. You certainly are not stingy. You are a good human being. But haven't we all fallen short? The Golden Rule comes to mind.

We are not talking about flattery. A genuine word of praise, given and received, can leave both persons feeling better. Compliments cost no money; we can all afford to give them. To withhold an encouraging word is stingy.

Sometimes we simply don't know how to say it. I hope these imaginary examples will spark an idea for what you might want to say:

How do you keep in such good shape?
You always seem to know the right thing to say.

This pesky diet of mine is hard on you, dear. I can't thank you enough. I owe you so much.

You are the best husband I could ever have found.

You are a wonderful daughter. I'm so proud of you.

I could not have done this without your help.

I'm a lucky guy to have the smartest agent in town.

I can't imagine a life without you.

No one can explain things better than you. You are a born teacher.

The world is a better place for having your kind in it.

You look like a movie star, but with more taste.

Everything goes better when you are here.

We can always depend on you. You are an angel.

TALKING ON THE TELEPHONE

What is more interesting than a telephone directory! Leafing through the yellow pages one day I saw numbers for Escort Services. Telling myself it was for research, I dialed one called Carolina Charm. Heard a soft "Hello" and then silence. The ball was in my court, and I had to hang up.

Looking at the yellow pages again, I selected Discreet Darlings and dialed. A business-like, no-nonsense voice said "Hello." I hung up fast. One more call, I told myself, and it would be enough research. This time I dialed Exotic Playmates, and got an answering machine. I didn't leave a message.

The tone of a Hello can make a difference in getting off to a good start. Women seem to be better at this than men. In fact, quite often men dispense with the greeting and say something like "Jones here." Or simply "Nash" as in the Nash Bridges series.

Let us consider a more important aspect of talking on the telephone: GETTING OFF THE PHONE. Sometimes we feel trapped. We want to be polite, but can't think of a tactful way to break off the conversation. What we need is a supply of kind and honest things to say. EXAMPLES:

I'm sorry, but I can't talk any longer. Please excuse me.

Forgive me, but I must get off the line. Gotta go!

So glad you called. Let's talk again soon. 'Bye now.

Always good to talk with you. Wish we had more time.

Please excuse me. There's something I must take care of.

I'm sorry, but this is not a good time for me to talk. Take care.

May I call you back? I'll have more time tomorrow.

Would you mind if we talked about this over lunch sometime?

Now you get the hang of it. The telephone is taking up many hours of our lives. Even on the beach we see people talking on their cellular phones. Perhaps holding a phone has taken the place left vacant by the cigarette.

Nowadays an answering machine is almost necessary. You will like it.

SPARKLING SPOUSAL CONVERSATION

My title suggests a very short essay. Couples in restaurants who are not conversing are judged to be married. The wife looks bored, and the husband looks bored.

But they may not be bored at all. They may be just tired. Let us imagine a baby-boomer couple who have determined never to give a bored impression in public. They play a game we can call Polishing the Wedding Ring.

Let's make up the game as we go along:

POLISHING THE WEDDING RING

HE: HERE'S LOOKING AT YOU, KID.
SHE: WE WILL ALWAYS HAVE PARIS.
HE: AND BUENOS AIRES.
SHE: BUENOS AIRES! I THOUGHT IT WAS CARACAS.
HE: WE WERE NEVER IN CARACAS.
SHE: DON'T YOU REMEMBER THE MATADOR?
HE: EL GUAPO? NO, I DON'T REMEMBER HIM.

SHE: HE FLIRTED WITH ME OUTRAGEOUSLY.

HE: SHOULD I GO BACK AND BEAT HIM UP?

SHE: NOT TILL AFTER DESSERT, DEAR.

HE: THOSE COLLEGE GIRLS ARE LOOKING AT US.

SHE: AT YOU. THEY THINK YOU ARE HANDSOME.

HE: DO YOU THINK I AM HANDSOME?

SHE: DEVASTATINGLY. BUT NOT LIKE EL GUAPO.

HE: YOU YEARN FOR A LATIN LOVER?

SHE: RIGHT NOW I YEARN FOR KEY LIME PIE.

HE: WE MUST GO BACK TO PARIS SOMETIME.

SHE: AND CARACAS.

Our couple look rested and happy as they leave the restaurant. The college girls stare. One of them sighs, "Didn't they just sparkle!"

IF YOU ARE

A. If you are an attractive single woman who is lonely and ready to settle down, you can do this: Read the local newspaper and find topics you can talk about. Start a friendly conversation in a safe place by asking an attractive man if he has seen the day's news. If he asks, "Why?" you can explain that you want the male perspective on an item. Pretend you are doing research and take notes. If a conversation begins, watch your language.

B. If you are an attractive single man who is lonely and ready to settle down, you can do this: Read the local newspaper and find topics you can talk about. Start a friendly conversation in a safe place by asking an attractive woman if she has seen the day's news. If she says "Why?" you can tell her that you want a woman's opinion on an item. If she seems willing to talk with you, you have an opening. But watch your language.

C. If you are a young man not ready to settle down but eager to make the acquaintance of attractive young women, you can do this: Read a local newspaper and learn about night classes, volunteer groups, guided tours, etc. Get out and see and be seen. Wear a T-shirt with your school name on it. Carry a plastic bag that announces a plea for the environment, and go around picking up trash. Try to look good, and if a girl speaks to you, have something pleasant to say. And watch your language.

D. If you are a young woman not ready to settle down but would enjoy some male companionship, you can do this: Read a local newspaper and learn about what is going on. Join church groups. Make girlfriends. Help elderly people. Smile and say "Hi" to strangers (in safe places) and look happy. Dare to speak to a nice looking person, male or female. You can ask "What do you think of this?" If an enjoyable conversation follows, it could lead to friendship. Of course you will watch your language.

E. If you are one of the above, you know what is meant by "watching your language." Even more important than grammar is clean speech. If you want to make a good impression, you will not use vulgar expressions. Dirty talk will hurt your chances. Profanity also. You don't want to scare people away. There is probably someone looking for you. Do your part. The right kind of language will help you.

TOPICS FOR A SOCIAL CONVERSATION

You find yourself in a situation you couldn't get out of. You have to entertain this stranger for two hours, and you have no idea what to talk about.

Having a meal together will help to pass the time, but sooner or later you will be expected to conduct a friendly conversation.

Let's try to think up some safe topics. It wouldn't hurt to make a list:

A. Is anything exciting going on over at your college?
B. Does your county have a county fair?
C. Is there much unemployment in your area?
D. Do you like to travel? Or take cruises?
E. Is your local newspaper liberal or conservative?
F. Do you have a favorite TV show?
G. Have you ever attended a rock concert?
H. Crafts are big now. Are you into anything?
I. Do you work out at a health club?
J. Do you have a favorite vacation spot?
K. Do you have your own Website? Do you use e-mail?

PART FOUR

HOW GOOD ARE YOU?

HOW GOOD ARE YOU?

TRUE OR FALSE

1. You speak distinctly. You do not swallow a final *r* and you do not drop the *g* in *ing* words/ Examples: *betta/better; sittin'/sitting.*
2. When you say *You guys*, it is never to females. When you say *You all*, it is never to just one person.
3. Everybody knows that *ain't* is not good grammar. Neither is *it don't.* You use them occasionally—but only for fun.
4. You say O*kay (OK)* quite often, but you try to vary it with other expressions, such as *Very well, Fine with me, Agreed, All right, Sure, No problem, Great, Perfect,* and *Quite satisfactory.*
5. You are quick with polite expressions such as *Please, Thank you, Excuse me, Beg your pardon,* and *Can I be of help?*
6. You have access to a good dictionary, and you use it often.
7. You have control over your vocabulary. You refrain from questionable language that might offend others.
8. You never say, "Aren't I?" You say, "Am I not?"

9. You do not like to hear, “Where’s it at?” You remember the smart-mouth answer, “Behind the AT.”
10. You know what they mean, but when otherwise bright people say, “I could care less,” you want to tell them it should be “could NOT care less.”

NOTE: There are 40 statements. If you find as many as 30 TRUE’s, you can give yourself an A+. *VERY* GOOD!

HOW GOOD ARE YOU?

11. Instead of the ubiquitous "like" you say "as"—in uses such as these: *Lance Armstrong won, as I thought he would; As the forecast indicated, the rain clouds moved in early; As I said, she's always late.*

12. You wish that more people would give up the LIKE habit and express themselves like these examples: *He's acting as though he hasn't seen us; She talks the way the finishing school taught her; I feel as if I might faint; It seems that nothing bothers him.*

13. Of course you would never start a sentence with, "Me and Henry." You could answer a question that way, politely changing it to "Henry and me."

14. You are aware that many well-educated people think it should be "Henry and I." But you know that this is a misconception. The form depends on whether this first-person pronoun is a subject or an object. (Forget Henry.)

15. You see something odd about expressions such as these: *What's with...; murder she wrote; Make nice; Enough already;* and *Not to worry.*

16. You remember from school books that a gerund is an "*ing*" verb-noun, as in "the running of the bulls." You know that it can take the possessive pronoun. That is why it sounds right to you to say: *Does my leaving early cause a problem?; Do your friends know about our losing all the luggage?;* and *I object to his smoking in the house.*

17. Is the word "*mother*" being replaced with "*mom*"? You have noticed the frequent use of "*mom.*" You decide that it is nothing to worry about.

18. You do not call a souvenir a "momento." The intended word is "memento."

19. You are familiar with *The Wizard of Oz* and can converse knowledgeably when people speak of following a yellow brick road, or not being in Kansas anymore, or paying no attention to the man behind the curtain. Dorothy and Toto, the tin man, the wicked witch—all part of this children's classic.

20. You would never modify the word "unique." Nothing is "very" unique.

21. You prefer "different from" to "different than."

22. Popular expressions become worn out. That is why you have given up asking, "Does that ring a bell?"

23. You know that "a choice" is not "two choices."
24. When you see TV shows such as "Judge Judy," you observe that a lot of people are deficient in grammar.
25. You can speak Spanish—or at least read some—and you are not averse to becoming more proficient.
26. "Minnie Pearl" said "How…dy!" and we loved her. You, however, know to say, "How do you do?"
27. People begin to notice if we use favorite words and expressions habitually. That is why you try not to get in a rut with words like *cool, neat, great, super, awesome, basically,* and *hopefully.*
28. You would never let "How come?" cross your lips.
29. You do not say "for real," "for sure," or "for free."
30. You would never say, "Did you eat yet?" You would say, "Have you eaten yet?"
31. You wish that writers would stop parroting "What- is- that- supposed- to- mean?" and simply write, "What does that mean?"
32. You agree that columnists should not use folksy words such as *gotta, gonna,* and *wanna.*

33. You would welcome a grass-roots movement dedicated to higher standards of speech.
34. You know if these verb forms are correct or incorrect:

YESTERDAY—*I done it, He saw us, We went there.*

MANY TIMES—*have did it, have seen, have went.*

35. You know to use "were" in "If I were you."
36. We often hear *lay* and *laying* instead of *lie* and *lying.* You never make this mistake.
37. You do not say an idea is *lousy* and you don't *buy it.*
38. The word *kids* is heard often. You prefer *children.*
39. You know when to say *Yes, ma'am* and *Yes, sir.*
40. English is a relatively new language. Before Shakespeare's plays, the court people in London spoke French. You are glad to know this.

AN APPEAL

To college students: Be sure you know the basics of English speech.

To teenagers: Read and listen. Strive to get a good vocabulary.

To executives: Agree to casual Fridays, but ask for formal Mondays in exchange. Not only formal attire but formal speech also. No slang.

To publishers: Establish a regular language feature. Be entertaining.

To universities: Provide leadership in organizing free language clinics.

To writers of soaps and sitcoms: Try not to perpetuate poor English. You do this when your characters recite lines using "lay" for "lie"; "like" for "as"; and "I" for "me." Let them correct themselves sometimes.

To awards givers: Add a special award and recognition for good grammar.

To governors: Insist that your state provide every opportunity possible for adults as well as children to learn basic English.

To public school teachers: Hang in there. Be careful with your own English. Attend language workshops.

To Congress: Please, honorable senators and representatives, do whatever you can to uphold the English language. Set a good example.

To parents and guardians: Accept the fact that English is difficult to learn, and don't be too proud to seek help.

To the President: Please consider enlarging your Cabinet to include a Secretary of the Language.

CONCLUSION

I haven't commented on Yiddish. Recently I have come across a number of Yiddish words. Leading them is *chutzpah*, which, by the way, is not pronounced the way it looks. William Safire has used it in *The NewYork Times,* thus giving it a stamp of approval. Other recognizable Yiddish words are *mensch, zaftig, schmooze,* and *schmuck.* Key Word players will find them in an American English dictionary.

Our language is a treasure that we enjoy every day, but take for granted. It deserves more attention. We must not let ourselves drift into a shorthand style of speech; *i.e. The State of the Union speech was neat. The President was real cool.*

I have been quite serious in this effort to point out areas of concern. Since "saying it right" means more than simply using acceptable grammar, I have included a few essays dealing with human relations. You can imagine my surprise when I received the e-mail letter printed below:

Dear Ms. Canter,

Thank you for your query and for your patience as I reviewed and discussed your proposal with our other editor on staff. We both thought the idea for your book was a good

> *one—and that it would probably be very funny. However, Coastal Carolina Press is not prepared to publish another collection of humor/Southern essays at this time.*

There was more, but you get the picture. In a way I was flattered. Humor? Southern? What do you think, dear readers?

Anyway I am happy with 1st BOOKS LIBRARY of Bloomington, Indiana. It has been a pleasure to work with them.

Special thanks to Tom.

ABOUT THE AUTHOR

Madge Myers Canter was born in 1913 in Sharpsburg, North Carolina to the reverend Charlie Myers and Addie Martin Myers. She attended high school in Mooresville, North Carolina and junior college in Mars Hill. In 1934, she received an A.B. degree from The University of North Carolina at Greensboro.

A teaching career followed, with positions in Brunswick, Rutherford and Anson counties. During various summer vacations she took courses at Appalachian State University, The University of North Carolina at Chapel Hill, and Duke University.

In 1947, she married Claude Canter of North Wilkesboro. During the 1960s and early '70s she taught English and Spanish at East Wilkes High School. In retirement she lives in North Myrtle Beach, South Carolina. In creating this "language aid for adults," she was assisted on the computer by her daughter, Claudia Marie Canter.

CPSIA information can be obtained at www.ICGtesting.com
Printed in the USA
BVOW071743250112

281380BV00001B/19/A

9 780759 691537